Times Tables & Multiplication Skills Activity Book

for ages 9-11

This CGP book is bursting with fun activities to build up children's skills and confidence.

It's ideal for extra practice to reinforce what they're learning in primary school. Enjoy!

Published by CGP

Editors:
Ruth Greenhalgh, Jake McGuffie, Sean McParland and Claire Plowman

With thanks to Alison Griffin and Caley Simpson for the proofreading.

With thanks to Jade Sim for the copyright research.

ISBN: 978 1 83774 070 3

Printed by Elanders Ltd, Newcastle upon Tyne.
Clipart on the cover and throughout the book from Corel®
Cover design concept by emc design ltd.

Text, design, layout and original illustrations © Coordination Group Publications Ltd. (CGP) 2024
All rights reserved.

Photocopying this book is not permitted, even if you have a CLA licence.
Extra copies are available from CGP with next day delivery • 0800 1712 712 • www.cgpbooks.co.uk

Contents

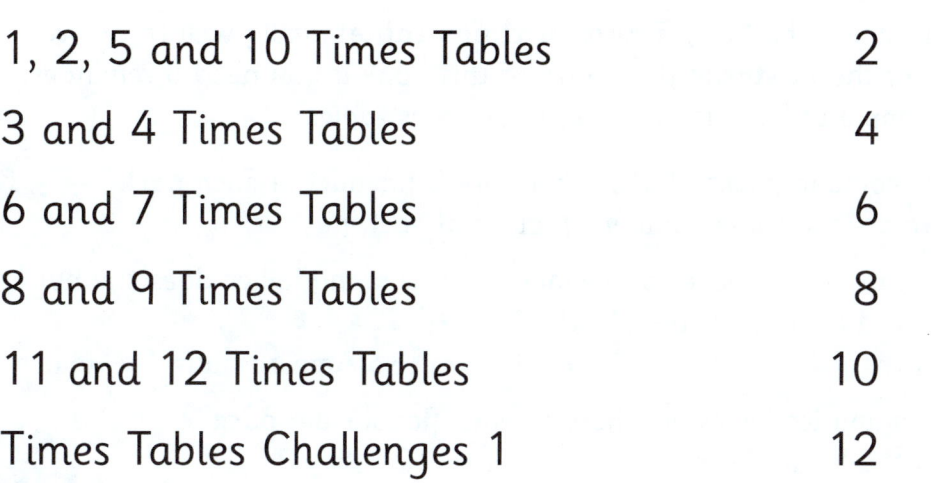

1, 2, 5 and 10 Times Tables	2
3 and 4 Times Tables	4
6 and 7 Times Tables	6
8 and 9 Times Tables	8
11 and 12 Times Tables	10
Times Tables Challenges 1	12

Poster: Factors and Multiples
Poster: Times Tables 1 to 12
Poster: Squares, Cubes and Primes

You can pull out these central pages to use them as a poster.

Times Tables Challenges 2	13
Mental Calculations	14
Factors and Multiples	16
Squares, Cubes and Primes	18
Written Methods	20
Puzzle: Race to the Bottom	22
Answers	24

1, 2, 5 and 10 Times Tables

How It Works

You'll need to know the **1, 2, 5 and 10 times tables** really well to answer these questions. Have a look at the **poster** in the centre of this book if you need a reminder. Here's an example of how you can use your times tables:

Ice lollies come in packs of 10. There are 5 flavours in each pack, and there are the same number of lollies of each flavour.

a) Ameera buys 11 packs of ice lollies. How many lollies does she buy in total?
   You need to find 11 lots of 10.
   From the 10 times table, 11 × 10 = 110, so Ameera buys 110 lollies.

b) How many ice lollies are there of each flavour per pack?
   From the 5 times table, 2 × 5 = 10, so 10 ÷ 5 = 2,
   so there are 2 lollies of each flavour.

Now Try These

1. Fill in the missing numbers in the calculations below.

   7 × ☐ = 35   120 ÷ 10 = ☐   ☐ × 2 = 22

   ☐ × 10 = 30   11 × ☐ = 11   60 ÷ ☐ = 12

   8 ÷ ☐ = 8   ☐ × 2 = 14   ☐ ÷ 10 = 7

2. Mark has 10 grandchildren. He divides £90 equally between them. How much money does each grandchild get?

   £ ....

3. Kath and Farid meet for lunch twice a month. How many times do they meet for lunch in a year?

   ....

4. Spike runs 100 miles in 10 weeks. Each of his runs is 5 miles long, and he goes for the same number of runs each week. How many runs does he go for each week?

....

5. Ding goes rowing for 2 hours at a time. He went rowing 10 times last month. At the end of each month, he puts a sticker in his training calendar for every 5 hours of rowing he did that month. How many stickers did he put in his calendar last month?

....

6. Lee has 8 identical buckets. Each bucket has a capacity of 5 litres. Lee also has 10 identical bottles. The total capacity of the bottles is the same as the total capacity of the buckets. What is the capacity of each bottle?

.... litres

7. In a flowerbed, there are 2 daffodil plants for every 5 crocus plants. There are 10 daffodil plants in total. How many crocus plants are there?

....

An Extra Challenge

Carla and Dewi have both been Christmas shopping for the same items. Their receipts are shown below, but some information is missing from Dewi's. Can you fill in Dewi's receipt? Note: the price per item is the same, no matter how many you buy.

Carla's receipt

2 candles	£12
10 baubles	£20
5 stockings	£45

Dewi's receipt

5 candles	£ ....
.... baubles	£14
2 stockings	£ ....

Have your times tables skills got 2, 5 or 10 times better?

3 and 4 Times Tables

How It Works

For the next couple of pages, it's the **3 and 4 times tables** that you'll need. They're on the times tables **poster**, so have a look there if you're feeling at all shaky on them. Read through these examples before you have a go at the questions:

It takes Harrison 3 minutes to paint a pattern onto a mug. How long will it take Harrison to paint 7 identical mugs?

From the 3 times table, 7 × 3 = 21, so it will take Harrison 21 minutes.

There are 36 children in a choir. The children stand in 4 rows, with the same number of children in each row. How many children are in each row?

From the 4 times table, 9 × 4 = 36.
So there are 36 ÷ 4 = 9 children in each row.

Now Try These

1. The masses of two items in an electrical shop are shown on the right.

    4 kg    3 kg

   Work out the total mass of:

   a) five vacuum cleaners   b) nine televisions   c) eleven vacuum cleaners

   .... kg   .... kg   .... kg

2. Fill in the missing numbers in the calculations below.

   ☐ × 3 = 24   40 ÷ ☐ = 10   ☐ ÷ 3 = 4

   4 × ☐ = 16   ☐ × 3 = 15   ☐ × 3 = 36

   18 ÷ 3 = ☐   7 × ☐ = 28   33 ÷ ☐ = 11

3. Lana has 48 eggs. She has some egg boxes that each hold 4 eggs. What is the smallest number of boxes she can put all the eggs into?

....

4. There are 24 penguins at a wildlife park.

   a) There are four times as many penguins as elephants. How many elephants are there?

   ....

   b) There are three penguins for every snake. How many snakes are there?

   ....

5. Four identical bunches of flowers cost £28. How much would three bunches cost?

   £ ....

An Extra Challenge

Apples and pears are sold in the packs shown below.

Sita says: I want to buy some packs of both types of fruit. I want to buy more than five packs of apples. I want to have 54 pieces of fruit in total.

How many packs of each type of fruit could she buy to give her everything she needs? How many other possible answers can you find?

How did it go? Tick a box be-four you move on...

6 and 7 Times Tables

How It Works

Now it's time for the **6 and 7 times tables**. Take a look at the times tables **poster** to jog your memory. Then make sure you understand how these examples work before diving into the questions:

Each episode of a cartoon lasts 7 minutes. How long will 5 episodes last?

From the 7 times table, 5 × 7 = 35, so 5 episodes last 35 minutes.

Karl bakes 60 doughnuts. He wants to put them into boxes of 6. How many boxes does he need?

From the 6 times table, 10 × 6 = 60, so Karl needs 60 ÷ 6 = 10 boxes.

Now Try These

1. **Circle** all the numbers that appear in the 6 times table.
   Draw a **rectangle** around all the numbers that appear in the 7 times table.

   63   14   32
        27   66
   45   77   36

2. Peggy and Dae always cut pizzas into the number of slices shown below.

   a) If Peggy cuts up 6 pizzas, how many slices will there be?

   ....

   Peggy **Dae**

   b) If Dae cuts up 8 pizzas, how many slices will there be?

   ....

3. It takes 7 hours to fly from the UK to Nigeria, and the same amount of time for the return trip. A pilot flies from the UK to Nigeria and back again twice in one week. How many hours do they spend flying?

   .... hours

4. Fill in the missing numbers in the calculations below.

   8 × ☐ = 56   9 × ☐ = 54   ☐ ÷ 6 = 12

   42 ÷ 6 = ☐   77 ÷ ☐ = 11   3 × ☐ = 21

   ☐ × 6 = 30   ☐ × 7 = 49   24 ÷ ☐ = 4

5. Maryam goes cycling every day for 70 days. How many weeks is this?

   .... weeks

6. In a school's PE cupboard, there are 6 footballs for every 7 tennis balls. There are 21 tennis balls in total. How many footballs are there?

   ....

An Extra Challenge

Olly has written some clues about the ages of his family members. How old is each person?

- My mum's age is in both the 6 and 7 times tables. She is older than me but younger than 80.

- My dad is older than 30 but more than a year younger than my mum. His age is in the 6 times table.

- My sister is 2 years younger than me. My age is in the 7 times table. My sister's age is below 20 and in the 6 times table.

Can you tackle any problem on the 6 or 7 times tables?

8 and 9 Times Tables

How It Works

You'll have to use your **8 and 9 times tables** to solve the problems on these pages. There's a lovely **poster** in the middle of the book if you need a reminder.
Here's a question that uses both the 8 and 9 times tables:

> For 11 days in a row, a journalist spent exactly 9 hours giving interviews and 8 hours sleeping. How many hours did she spend doing each activity in total?

Read the question carefully, and use your times tables to work out the answers.
She spent 11 × 9 = 99 hours giving interviews and 11 × 8 = 88 hours sleeping.

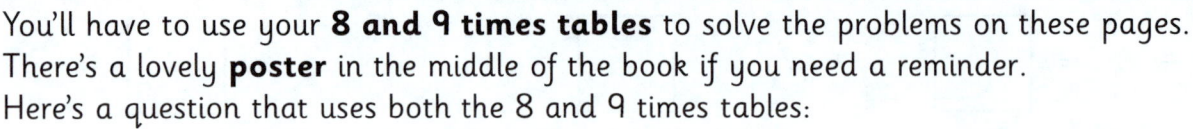

Now Try These

1. Cross out the number that is in **neither** the 8 nor the 9 times table.

2. Next year, Jesminder wants to climb as many hills as she can. How many hills will she climb in total if she climbs...

   a) 8 new hills each month?

   ....

   b) 9 new hills each month?

   ....

3. A library book is made up of 9 chapters.
   There are the same number of pages in each chapter.
   There are 81 pages in the book in total.
   How many pages are there in each chapter?

   ....

4. Fill in the missing numbers in the calculations below.

   3 × 8 = ☐   10 × 9 = ☐   ☐ × 8 = 16

   ☐ × 9 = 54   24 ÷ ☐ = 3   27 ÷ 9 = ☐

   64 ÷ 8 = ☐   9 × 9 = ☐   ☐ × 8 = 88

5. David wants to buy some new notepads. At the stationery shop, one notepad costs £8. David has £45 to spend on notepads. What is the largest number of notepads that David can afford?

....

6. Aldo is giving a speech at a local charity event. After every 9 lines of his speech that he reads out, he takes a sip of water.

   a) After reading 63 lines, how many sips has Aldo taken in total?

   ....

   b) By his 8th sip of water, how many lines has he read?

   ....

An Extra Challenge

Lulu Winmore and Oleg Neverlost are long-standing rivals at the annual TeeVee Awards. Draw lines to match the awards to the correct winner, cross out any that neither of them win, and circle the one they'll need to share.

"I only want numbers you can get by multiplying an **odd** number by 8, please."

"I only want numbers you can get by multiplying an **even** number by 9, thanks."

56, 94, 40, 72, 36, 28

Did you get on famously well with these problems?

 ☐   ☐   ☐   ☐

11 and 12 Times Tables

How It Works

These problems involve the **11 times table** and the **12 times table**. Have a look at the **poster** in the middle of this book before you start, then crack on with this example question:

> At the sweet shop, each member of the Bernstein family buys 11 lollipops, and each member of the Stuart family buys 12 lollipops. There are 9 people in the Bernstein family and 8 people in the Stuart family. Which family buys more lollipops?

There are 9 Bernstein family members, and each buys 11 lollipops.
This is 9 × 11 = 99 lollipops in total.

There are 8 Stuart family members, and each buys 12 lollipops.
This is 8 × 12 = 96 lollipops in total.

99 is more than 96, so the Bernstein family buys more lollipops.

Now Try These

1. Fill in the missing numbers in the calculations below.

   5 × 11 = ☐   11 × 12 = ☐   ☐ × 11 = 66

   ☐ × 12 = 60   ☐ ÷ 12 = 7   24 ÷ ☐ = 2

   11 × ☐ = 121   108 ÷ 12 = ☐   96 ÷ 12 = ☐

2. Joy goes to pick fruit from her village's orchard. She picks all the fruit from three orange trees, which each have twelve oranges on them.

   a) How many oranges does she pick?

   ....

   b) The pear trees in the orchard each have eleven pears on them.
   Joy picks all the fruit from four pear trees.
   How many **more** pears than oranges does Joy pick?

   ....

10

3. Min-jun makes £77 by selling 11 Min-jun costumes.
   Each costume costs the same amount.
   How much do 12 costumes cost?

£ ....

4. Martha makes grape juice from the grapes in her vineyard.
   The last batch produced 130 bottles, and she wants to pack them all into crates.
   Each crate can hold 12 bottles. How many crates will Martha need?

   ....

5. Bob is putting some salt and vinegar on his fish and chips.

   a) There are 48 chips. He uses 1 pinch of salt per 12 chips.
      How many pinches of salt does he use?

   ....

   b) The fish is 33 cm long. He uses 12 drops of vinegar
      per 11 cm of fish. How many drops of vinegar does he use?

   ....

An Extra Challenge

Shelly and Mollie are always in competition with each other, but time and time again Mollie comes out on top. For every 11 things Shelly has, Mollie has 12.
Fill in the missing numbers in their statements.

I've got £22 in my purse! — Well I have £ .... in mine.

I got .... birthday gifts. — That's nothing, I got 144.

I have 44 friends. — Good for you, I have .... !

Shelly   Mollie

Did these problems put up much of a fight?

Times Tables Challenges 1

How It Works

Now you've got all your times tables nailed, it's time to take things up a notch. Use your times tables knowledge to tackle these multiplication and division problems.

Now Try These

1. Edie has 54 equal-sized fabric squares. She sews sets of them together to make larger squares which are all the same size. If she uses all her squares, how many large squares does she make? How many small squares make up each large square?
   Hint: start by looking for the possible numbers of small squares in each large square.

   .... large squares made up of .... small squares each

2. Thomasina the terrapin and Hugo the hare are having a race.
   Use the information below to work out who gets to the finish line first.

   | Thomasina cheats. She divides the race into equal legs and gets her 6 cousins to take one leg each, then runs the final one herself. |

   The race is 84 m long.

   Hugo runs 12 m every 11 seconds.   Each terrapin takes 9 seconds to run their leg.

   ....

3. There are 8 cars in a race. At a pit stop, crew members use wheel guns and wheel jacks to change all four tyres on a car. Each car has its own crew and equipment.
   Use these boxes to work out the totals below for carrying out a pit stop on all 8 cars.

   3 seconds **per car**   2 crew members at **each end** of **each car**

   2 crew members **per wheel**   2 wheel guns **per wheel**   2 wheel jacks **per car**

   .... pieces of equipment in total   .... crew members in total   .... seconds of work in total

Factors and Multiples

Factors

Factors are all the whole numbers that divide a number exactly.
Here's how to find the factors of 12:

　　Just list all the pairs of numbers that make 12.
　　So the factors of 12 are **1, 2, 3, 4, 6** and **12**.

$1 \times 12 = 12$
$2 \times 6 = 12$
$3 \times 4 = 12$

Prime Factors

These are just factors which are prime.
The prime factors of 12 are **2** and **3**.

1, **2**, **3**, 4, 6 and 12

Only 2 and 3 are prime numbers.

Common Factors

A common factor is a factor that two or more numbers share.

Compare the factors of two numbers to find the ones they have in common.

The common factors of 12 and 16 are **1, 2** and **4**.

1, 2, 3, **4**, 6 and 12

1, 2, 4, 8 and 16

These are the factors of 16.

Multiples

Multiples of a number are what you get if you multiply that number by whole numbers.
So the multiples of 6 are just the numbers in the 6 times table and beyond:

6	12	18	24	30	36	42	48	54	60	66	72 ...
×1	×2	×3	×4	×5	×6	×7	×8	×9	×10	×11	×12

Common Multiples

A common multiple is a multiple that two or more numbers share.

Compare the multiples of two numbers to find the ones they have in common.

The first four common multiples of 8 and 12 are **24, 48, 72** and **96**.

The multiples of 8 are:
8　16　**24**　32　40　**48**
56　64　**72**　80　88　**96** ...

The multiples of 12 are:
12　**24**　36　**48**　60　**72**　84　**96** ...

Times Tab[le]

1 Times Table
0 × 1 = 0
1 × 1 = 1
2 × 1 = 2
3 × 1 = 3
4 × 1 = 4
5 × 1 = 5
6 × 1 = 6
7 × 1 = 7
8 × 1 = 8
9 × 1 = 9
10 × 1 = 10
11 × 1 = 11
12 × 1 = 12

2 Times Table
0 × 2 = 0
1 × 2 = 2
2 × 2 = 4
3 × 2 = 6
4 × 2 = 8
5 × 2 = 10
6 × 2 = 12
7 × 2 = 14
8 × 2 = 16
9 × 2 = 18
10 × 2 = 20
11 × 2 = 22
12 × 2 = 24

3 Times Table
0 × 3 = 0
1 × 3 = 3
2 × 3 = 6
3 × 3 = 9
4 × 3 = 12
5 × 3 = 15
6 × 3 = 18
7 × 3 = 21
8 × 3 = 24
9 × 3 = 27
10 × 3 = 30
11 × 3 = 33
12 × 3 = 36

7 Times Table
0 × 7 = 0
1 × 7 = 7
2 × 7 = 14
3 × 7 = 21
4 × 7 = 28
5 × 7 = 35
6 × 7 = 42
7 × 7 = 49
8 × 7 = 56
9 × 7 = 63
10 × 7 = 70
11 × 7 = 77
12 × 7 = 84

8 Times Table
0 × 8 = 0
1 × 8 = 8
2 × 8 = 16
3 × 8 = 24
4 × 8 = 32
5 × 8 = 40
6 × 8 = 48
7 × 8 = 56
8 × 8 = 64
9 × 8 = 72
10 × 8 = 80
11 × 8 = 88
12 × 8 = 96

9 Times Table
0 × 9 = 0
1 × 9 = 9
2 × 9 = 18
3 × 9 = 27
4 × 9 = 36
5 × 9 = 45
6 × 9 = 54
7 × 9 = 63
8 × 9 = 72
9 × 9 = 81
10 × 9 = 90
11 × 9 = 99
12 × 9 = 108

© CGP — not to be photocopied

es 1 to 12

4 Times Table
0 × 4 = 0
1 × 4 = 4
2 × 4 = 8
3 × 4 = 12
4 × 4 = 16
5 × 4 = 20
6 × 4 = 24
7 × 4 = 28
8 × 4 = 32
9 × 4 = 36
10 × 4 = 40
11 × 4 = 44
12 × 4 = 48

5 Times Table
0 × 5 = 0
1 × 5 = 5
2 × 5 = 10
3 × 5 = 15
4 × 5 = 20
5 × 5 = 25
6 × 5 = 30
7 × 5 = 35
8 × 5 = 40
9 × 5 = 45
10 × 5 = 50
11 × 5 = 55
12 × 5 = 60

6 Times Table
0 × 6 = 0
1 × 6 = 6
2 × 6 = 12
3 × 6 = 18
4 × 6 = 24
5 × 6 = 30
6 × 6 = 36
7 × 6 = 42
8 × 6 = 48
9 × 6 = 54
10 × 6 = 60
11 × 6 = 66
12 × 6 = 72

10 Times Table
0 × 10 = 0
1 × 10 = 10
2 × 10 = 20
3 × 10 = 30
4 × 10 = 40
5 × 10 = 50
6 × 10 = 60
7 × 10 = 70
8 × 10 = 80
9 × 10 = 90
10 × 10 = 100
11 × 10 = 110
12 × 10 = 120

11 Times Table
0 × 11 = 0
1 × 11 = 11
2 × 11 = 22
3 × 11 = 33
4 × 11 = 44
5 × 11 = 55
6 × 11 = 66
7 × 11 = 77
8 × 11 = 88
9 × 11 = 99
10 × 11 = 110
11 × 11 = 121
12 × 11 = 132

12 Times Table
0 × 12 = 0
1 × 12 = 12
2 × 12 = 24
3 × 12 = 36
4 × 12 = 48
5 × 12 = 60
6 × 12 = 72
7 × 12 = 84
8 × 12 = 96
9 × 12 = 108
10 × 12 = 120
11 × 12 = 132
12 × 12 = 144

cgpbooks.co.uk

Squares, Cubes and Primes

Squares

$1^2 = 1 \times 1 = 1$
$2^2 = 2 \times 2 = 4$
$3^2 = 3 \times 3 = 9$
$4^2 = 4 \times 4 = 16$
$5^2 = 5 \times 5 = 25$
$6^2 = 6 \times 6 = 36$
$7^2 = 7 \times 7 = 49$
$8^2 = 8 \times 8 = 64$
$9^2 = 9 \times 9 = 81$
$10^2 = 10 \times 10 = 100$
$11^2 = 11 \times 11 = 121$
$12^2 = 12 \times 12 = 144$

Cubes

$1^3 = 1 \times 1 \times 1 = 1$
$2^3 = 2 \times 2 \times 2 = 8$
$3^3 = 3 \times 3 \times 3 = 27$
$4^3 = 4 \times 4 \times 4 = 64$
$5^3 = 5 \times 5 \times 5 = 125$

Primes

A **prime number** is a number with exactly 2 factors: 1 and itself.

1	②	③	4	⑤	6	⑦	8	9	10
⑪	12	⑬	14	15	16	⑰	18	⑲	20
21	22	㉓	24	25	26	27	28	㉙	30
㉛	32	33	34	35	36	㊲	38	39	40
㊶	42	㊸	44	45	46	㊼	48	49	50
51	52	㊾	54	55	56	57	58	㊾	60
㊿	62	63	64	65	66	㊸	68	69	70
㊟	72	㊷	74	75	76	77	78	㊾	80
81	82	㊸	84	85	86	87	88	㊾	90
91	92	93	94	95	96	㊾	98	99	100

Primes circled: 2, 3, 5, 7, 11, 13, 17, 19, 23, 29, 31, 37, 41, 43, 47, 53, 59, 61, 67, 71, 73, 79, 83, 89, 97.

Times Tables Challenges 2

How It Works

Pull all those times tables out of the hat and mix them up for some more multiplication and division challenges. Now then, abracadabra, one, two, three...

Now Try These

1. Winifred is scaling her potion recipe for three different sizes of cauldron.
   Fill in the missing numbers to show how many of each ingredient is in each cauldron.
   Hint: use the numbers of frog legs to work out how much to scale the other numbers by.

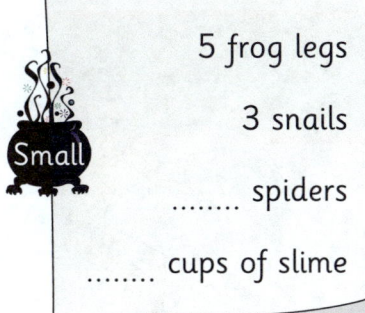

Small
- 5 frog legs
- 3 snails
- .... spiders
- .... cups of slime

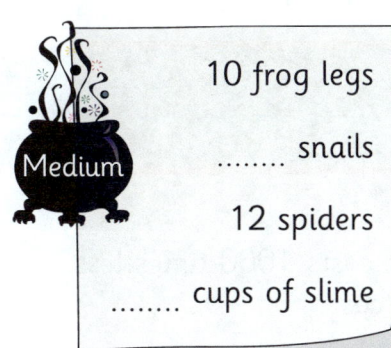

Medium
- 10 frog legs
- .... snails
- 12 spiders
- .... cups of slime

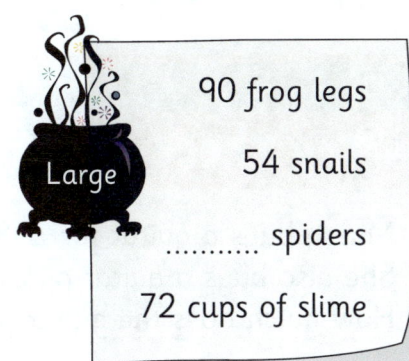

Large
- 90 frog legs
- 54 snails
- .... spiders
- 72 cups of slime

2. a) At a fair, one roller coaster has 6-seat cars and another has 7-seat cars.
   Each roller coaster has the same maximum capacity and has fewer than 12 cars.
   What is the maximum capacity of each roller coaster?

   .... people

   b) Macy, Khalid and Joe rode different numbers of roller coasters at the fair.
   Each person rode each of their chosen roller coasters a certain number of times.
   Each ride on a roller coaster cost **2 tokens**, and each person spent 60 tokens on riding roller coasters. Fill in the missing numbers below.

   Macy rode [ ] different roller coasters 6 times each.

   Khalid rode [ ] different roller coasters 3 times each.

   Joe rode [ ] different roller coasters 5 times each.

Mental Calculations

How It Works

These pages are on mental calculations, so work out the answers in your head. You'll need to tackle them in a few different ways, depending on the question.

Multiply or divide by 10, 100 and 1000 by shifting digits — to the left for multiplication, to the right for division.

E.g. 0.25 × 10 = 2.5
Move the digits one place to the left.

Split harder calculations up, either by doing an easier calculation first, or by using addition and subtraction. Here are a couple of examples:

20 × 4000 — do 2 × 4, then add the four zeroes at the end: 2 × 4 = 8. So 20 × 4000 = **80 000**.

71 × 8 — split 71 up, multiply each part by 8, then add them back together:

71 = 70 + 1
70 × 8 = 560
1 × 8 = 8
So 71 × 8 = 560 + 8 = **568**.

Now Try These

1. Mazzy buys a guitar for £980.
   She also buys a guitar pick that costs 1000 times less.
   How much does the guitar pick cost?

   £ ....

2. Work out the answers to these calculations.

   40 × 9 =

   1080 ÷ 12 =

   660 ÷ 11 =

   600 × 7 =

   50 × 90 =

   720 ÷ 80 =

3. One very smart baboon is writing a novel.
   Every time it finishes writing 1.2 pages, it treats itself to a banana.
   How many pages has the baboon written when it gets its 11th banana?

   Banana Karenina

   ....

4. Hakim orders 94 ribbons, one for each of his dogs. Each ribbon costs £7. How much do they cost altogether?

£ ....

5. Stink About It, the candle factory in Cheeseville, makes 480 parmesan-scented candles every hour. How many parmesan-scented candles does the factory make in 10 minutes?

....

6. a) There are 10 cans of King Soda in one box. How many cans are there in 18 boxes?

....

b) There are 10 boxes of King Soda in one crate. How many cans are there in 32 crates?

....

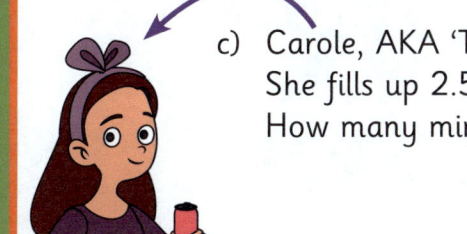

c) Carole, AKA 'The Beast', works in the King Soda factory. She fills up 2.5 cans of King Soda every minute. How many minutes does it take her to fill up a crate's worth of cans?

.... minutes

An Extra Challenge

Robo-Brain has spat out one of his number facts again.

$0.042 \times 6785 = 284.97$

Use Robo-Brain's fact, plus your mental maths skills, to solve the following problems.

$42 \times 6785 = ?$

$6.785 \times 4.2 = ?$

$0.042 \times 6784 = ?$

$0.042 \times 1 \times 6785 = ?$

$2849.7 \div 6785 = ?$

How's your brain after all that? Tick a box, if you don't mind...

Factors and Multiples

How It Works

The **factors** of a number are all the whole numbers that divide it exactly.

The **factors** of 6 are **1, 2, 3** and **6**.

The **multiples** of a number are what you get by multiplying that number by whole numbers.

The **multiples** of 4 are **4, 8, 12, 16**, ...

There's a **poster** in the middle of the book that covers factors and multiples in more detail, so make sure to give it a look for a proper recap.

Now Try These

1. This list shows all but one of the factors of 18.

   Which factor is missing from the list?

   ....

2. a) Write down the first five multiples of 9.

   ....

   b) Find the **lowest** common multiple of 9 and 12.

   ....

3. Fill in the gaps to complete these factor pairs of 54.

   1, ☐   2, ☐   ☐, 18   ☐, 9

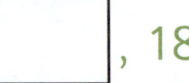

4. Astrid is thinking of a number. She says, "the number I'm thinking of is a common factor of 9 and all numbers in the 6 times table, but it isn't the number 1." What number is Astrid thinking of?

....

5. How many factors of 132 are also multiples of 11?

....

6. Kian writes down the problem on the right. Circle **all** the options below that give the same answer as Kian's problem. Hint: use the factor pairs of 12 and 22 to help.

$12 \times 22 = ?$

| $2 \times 3 \times 66$ | $3 \times 4 \times 2 \times 11$ | $4 \times 6 \times 11$ | $4 \times 2 \times 44$ |

7. A troll stops you as cross over his bridge. "You must solve my riddle to pass", he says. "I have a pretty smile — on the top row of teeth, there's a tooth for every multiple of 4 between 30 and 50. On the bottom row, there are two teeth for every multiple of 7 less than 30. How many teeth do I have in total?"

....

An Extra Challenge

You are bearing witness to the world premiere of Marcel the Mathmagician's newest (and worst) trick.

First, his daredevil assistant Fiona Actor says a number. Then, Marcel saws Fiona in half, and the boxes reveal a factor pair of Fiona's number. The boxes never show the number that Fiona says. Now, on with the trick...

Fiona says an odd number less than 150, and SHAZAM! **Both** magic boxes show the **same number**...

Fiona says the same number again, and WHOOSH! A **different** factor pair appears...

What number did Fiona say?

Did you find all this tricky? Or did it work like magic?

Squares, Cubes and Primes

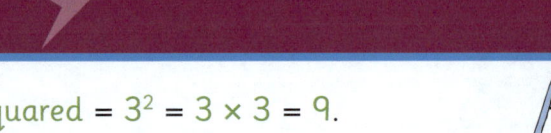

How It Works

To **square** a number, multiply it by itself, e.g. 3 squared = 3^2 = 3 × 3 = 9.
9 is a **square number** because you can make it by multiplying the number 3 by itself.

To **cube** a number, multiply it by itself then by itself again, e.g. 4 cubed = 4 × 4 × 4 = 64.
64 is a **cube number**.

A **prime number** has only **two factors** — itself and 1. It can't be divided by any other number. You can find the **prime factors** of a number by using a factor tree. For example:

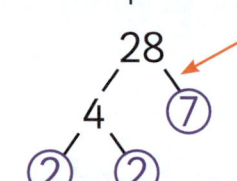

Find a pair of factors, and keep splitting into factor pairs until the numbers won't split any further, i.e. they are prime numbers.

The circled numbers are prime factors.
28 = 2 × 2 × 7

See the **poster** in the middle of this book for more on squares, cubes, primes and prime factors.

Now Try These

1. In Jamal's school tombola, you pick a ticket from a barrel to try to win a prize. You win a prize if you pick a ticket that shows the square of the number on the prize. What would the winning tickets be for each of the prizes below?

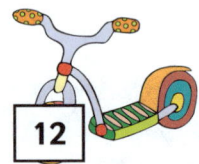

Microphone: ....   Rabbit: ....   Scooter: ....

2. At Prime Time Bowling, there are 100 bowling pins to aim for. You get a special prize for knocking down a prime number of pins.

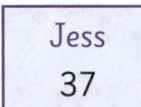

   a) The numbers of pins that 5 children knocked down are shown below. Circle all the children who would get a special prize.

Jess	Phil	Rupa	Liam	Chidi
37	39	59	23	67

   b) How many special prizes are available for knocking down fewer than 20 pins?

   ....

   c) What is the biggest number of pins that would get a special prize?

   ....

3. Complete these factor trees.

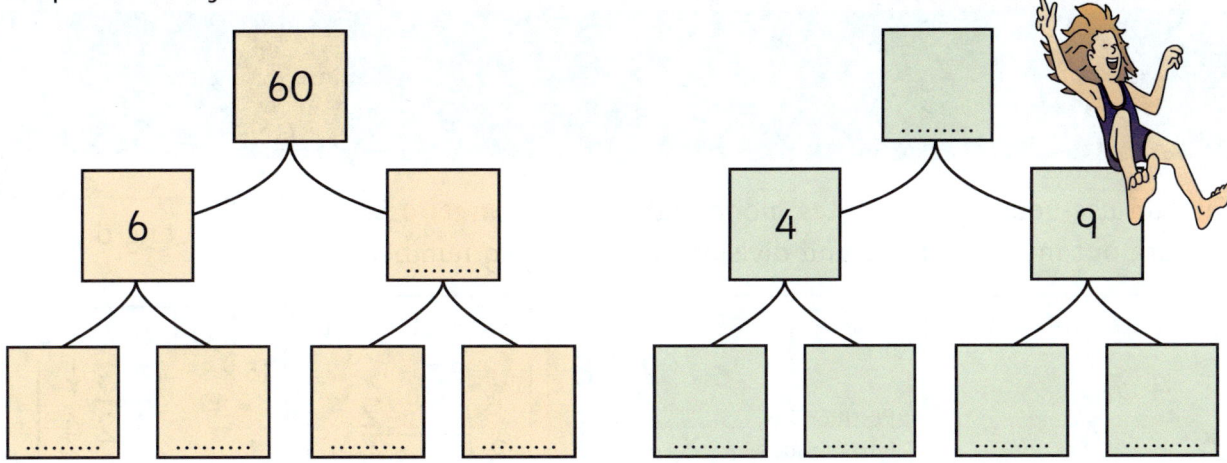

4. Jasmin is packing tennis balls into boxes. She uses square trays in the sizes shown.

   a) Complete the calculations to show how many tennis balls can fit in each tray.

   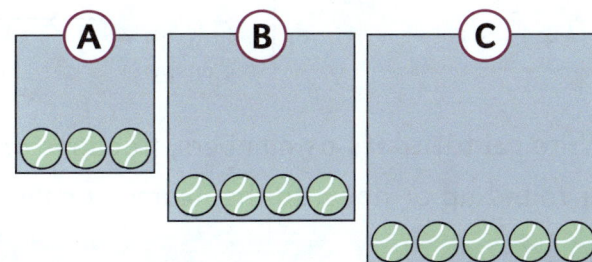

   A: 3^2 = ... B: .... = 16 C: 5^2 = ...

   b) Jasmin always stacks up full trays of the same size (A, B or C), in such a way that the number of balls in each stack is a cube number. If she packs 145 balls into stacks of trays, with no balls left over, how many of each tray size does she use?

   A: .... B: .... C: ....

An Extra Challenge

Use the clues below to find the mystery number.

| I am between 2^3 and 3^3. |

| I am one more than a prime number. |

| $\frac{1}{3}$ of my factors are prime. |

| I do **not** have a prime factor of 3. |

| If you square me, you'll get a number bigger than 100. |

Are you primed and ready for anything in this topic?

Written Methods

How It Works

You can use your **times tables** along with **written methods** to work out multiplications and divisions involving big numbers.

Short multiplication

```
    4 3 6
  ×     4
  -------
  1 7 4 4
    1 2
```
6 × 4 = 24
3 × 4 = 12
12 + 2 = 14
4 × 4 = 16
16 + 1 = 17

Long multiplication

```
          2 7 8
  ×         3 6
  -------------
278 × 6 → 1 6 6 8
            4 4
278 × 30→ 8 3 4 0
            2 2
Add to get→1 0 0 0 8
the answer.   1 1
```
Partition 36 into 6 and 30.

Short division

7 ÷ 3 = 2 r1
```
     2 6 2
  3 )7 ¹8 ⁶6
```
18 ÷ 3 = 6
6 ÷ 3 = 2

Long division

```
           3 8 2 r 12
       15 )5 7 4 2
15 × 3   − 4 5
 = 45    -------
           1 2 4
15 × 8   − 1 2 0
 = 120   -------
               4 2
15 × 2   −    3 0
 = 30    -------
               1 2
```
The remainder is 12.

Write **remainders** as numbers, fractions or decimals. → 215 ÷ 4 = 53 r 3 or 53$\frac{3}{4}$ or 53.75
Or round up or down to the nearest whole number depending on the context of the question.

Now Try These

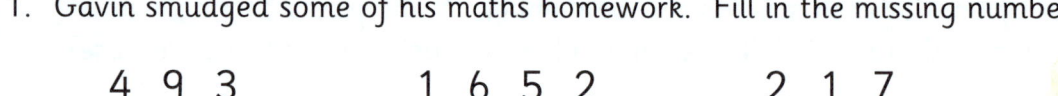

1. Gavin smudged some of his maths homework. Fill in the missing numbers.

```
    4 9 3          1 6 5 2          2 1 7          ..... 7 8
  ×     8        ×       7        ×   .....      ×       6
  -------        ---------        ---------      -----------
 ..........     ............       ..... 6 8       5 2 .....
```

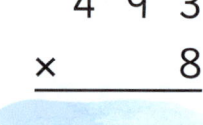

2. Sophie is organising a music festival. She sells 5252 adult tickets and 4519 child tickets.

   a) She needs to provide one staff member for every 8 children. How many staff members does she need?

   b) She needs to have one shower for every 12 adults. How many showers should she hire?

....

3. Carly is a lumberjack. The trees on the plantation she works at are arranged in 68 rows of 380.

   a) How many trees are in the plantation?

   ....

   b) She's asked to harvest $\frac{1}{8}$ of the trees. How many trees should she cut down?

   ....

   c) Each truck used to transport the trees can carry 20 trees. How many trucks will Carly need to transport all the trees she has cut down?

   ....

   d) The trees are sawn into shorter logs. One tree is 2253 cm tall and is cut into 3 equal lengths. How long is each log?

   .... cm

   e) The logs are split into slices, 16 mm thick. If the log is 386 mm thick, how many slices can be cut? Write the remainder as a fraction.

   ....

An Extra Challenge

The maths monster has left a secret message. Crack the code to work out what she says.

A	B	C	D	E	F	G	H	I	J	K	L	M
1	11	17	18	0	12	9	3	14	19	2	4	5
N	O	P	Q	R	S	T	U	V	W	X	Y	Z
15	6	20	22	7	24	13	8	16	21	23	10	25

(___ ___) ___ ___ ___   (___ ___ ___ ___) ___   (___ ___)!

714 ÷ 14
221 ÷ 17
the remainder from 3891 ÷ 8
288 ÷ 12
28 × 280
216 ÷ 9
1984 ÷ 32

Did you divide and conquer written methods?

Race to the Bottom

It's the annual Downhill Dash in Frostria! Complete each player's info card, then use the **final place hint** with their info to work out the place they finished in the race. Write their names in the **Final Results** box to show the order in which they crossed the line.

Boardan Mittens
Age: 15

Fun fact: I've practised at least once a week over the past year. The number of days I've practised is a square number that's also a cube number. That's...

.... days

Final place hint: the ones digit

Snophelia Frost
Age: 31

Fun fact: My gran is the oldest to ever win the Dash. At the time, her age was equal to the 5th smallest prime number squared, which is...

.... years old

Final place hint: the tens digit

Max Speed
Age: 22

Fun fact: I won 14 races last year, each with a cash prize of £275, earning a grand total of...

£ ....

Final place hint: the thousands digit

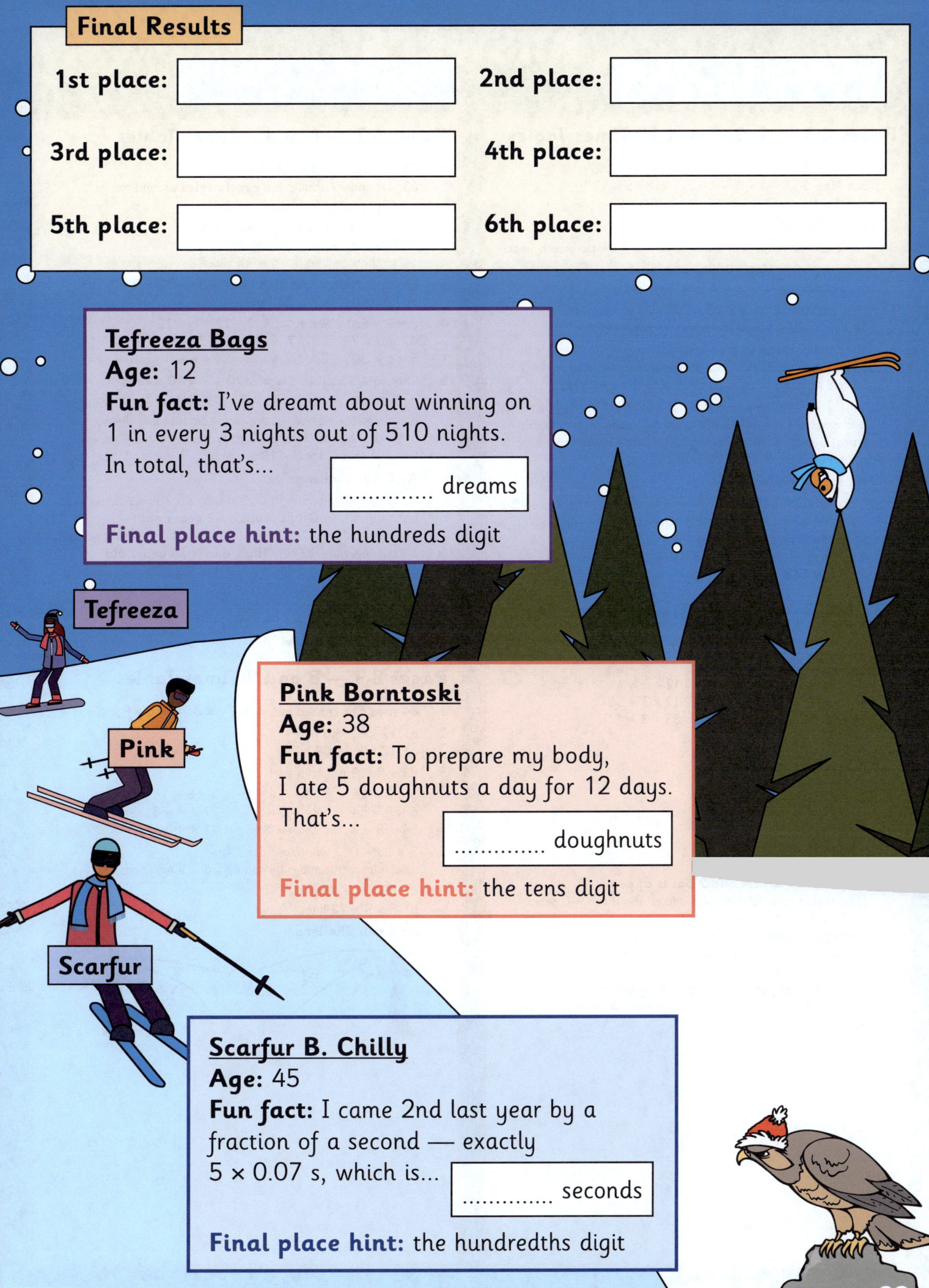

Final Results

1st place: _____ 2nd place: _____

3rd place: _____ 4th place: _____

5th place: _____ 6th place: _____

Tefreeza Bags
Age: 12
Fun fact: I've dreamt about winning on 1 in every 3 nights out of 510 nights. In total, that's…
………… dreams
Final place hint: the hundreds digit

Pink Borntoski
Age: 38
Fun fact: To prepare my body, I ate 5 doughnuts a day for 12 days. That's…
………… doughnuts
Final place hint: the tens digit

Scarfur B. Chilly
Age: 45
Fun fact: I came 2nd last year by a fraction of a second — exactly 5 × 0.07 s, which is…
………… seconds
Final place hint: the hundredths digit

Answers

Pages 2-3 — 1, 2, 5 and 10 Times Tables

1. 7 × **5** = 35   120 ÷ 10 = **12**   11 × 2 = 22
    3 × 10 = 30   11 × **1** = 11   60 ÷ **5** = 12
    8 ÷ **1** = 8   7 × 2 = 14   **70** ÷ 10 = 7
2. £90 ÷ 10 = **£9**
3. There are 12 months in a year.   12 × 2 = **24** times in a year.
4. He runs 100 ÷ 10 = 10 miles each week.
    So he goes for 10 ÷ 5 = **2** runs each week.
5. He went rowing for 2 × 10 = 20 hours last month.
    So he put 20 ÷ 5 = **4** stickers in his calendar.
6. The total capacity of the buckets is 8 × 5 = 40 litres,
    so the total capacity of the bottles is also 40 litres.
    So the capacity of each bottle is 40 ÷ 10 = **4 litres**.
7. 10 ÷ 2 = 5, so the number of daffodil plants in the flowerbed
    is 5 times the number in the ratio. So multiply the number of
    crocus plants in the ratio by 5 to find how many there are in
    the flowerbed: 5 × 5 = **25** crocus plants.

    An Extra Challenge
    1 candle costs £12 ÷ 2 = £6, so 5 candles cost £6 × 5 = **£30**.
    1 bauble costs £20 ÷ 10 = £2. Dewi paid £14 for baubles,
    so he must have bought £14 ÷ £2 = **7** baubles.
    1 stocking costs £45 ÷ 5 = £9, so 2 stockings cost
    £9 × 2 = **£18**.

Pages 4-5 — 3 and 4 Times Tables

1. a) 5 × 4 kg = **20 kg**   b) 9 × 3 kg = **27 kg**
    c) 11 × 4 kg = **44 kg**
2. 8 × 3 = 24   40 ÷ **4** = 10   12 ÷ 3 = 4
    4 × 4 = 16   5 × 3 = 15   12 × 3 = 36
    18 ÷ 3 = **6**   7 × **4** = 28   33 ÷ **3** = 11
3. 48 ÷ 4 = **12** boxes
4. a) 24 ÷ 4 = **6** elephants
    b) 24 ÷ 3 = **8** snakes
5. 1 bunch costs £28 ÷ 4 = £7,
    so 3 bunches would cost £7 × 3 = **£21**.

    An Extra Challenge
    Sita could buy:
    12 packs of apples and 2 packs of pears
    (This would give 12 × 4 = 48 apples and 2 × 3 = 6 pears,
    so 48 + 6 = 54 pieces of fruit.)
    9 packs of apples and 6 packs of pears
    (This would give 9 × 4 = 36 apples and 6 × 3 = 18 pears,
    so 36 + 18 = 54 pieces of fruit.)
    6 packs of apples and 10 packs of pears
    (This would give 6 × 4 = 24 apples and 10 × 3 = 30 pears,
    so 24 + 30 = 54 pieces of fruit.)

Pages 6-7 — 6 and 7 Times Tables

1. **66** and **36** should be **circled**.
    63, **14** and **77** should have **rectangles** around them.
2. a) Peggy cuts pizzas into 7 slices,
       so there will be 6 × 7 = **42** slices.
    b) Dae cuts pizzas into 6 slices,
       so there will be 8 × 6 = **48** slices.
3. Flying to Nigeria and back twice will take 2 × 2 = 4 lots
    of 7 hours. 4 × 7 = **28 hours**.
4. 8 × 7 = 56   9 × **6** = 54   72 ÷ 6 = 12
    42 ÷ 6 = **7**   77 ÷ **7** = 11   3 × **7** = 21
    5 × 6 = 30   7 × 7 = 49   24 ÷ **6** = 4
5. There are 7 days in a week. 70 ÷ 7 = **10 weeks**.
6. 21 ÷ 7 = 3, so the number of tennis balls in the cupboard
    is 3 times the number in the ratio. So multiply the number
    of footballs in the ratio by 3 to find how many there are in
    the cupboard: 3 × 6 = **18** footballs.

    An Extra Challenge
    42 is the only number in both the 6 and 7 times tables that is
    less than 80, so **Olly's mum** is **42 years old**.
    36 is the only number in the 6 times table that is more than
    30 but less than 42, so **Olly's dad** is **36 years old**.
    Olly's age is in the 7 times table and less than 42. Olly's
    sister's age is less than 20, in the 6 times table and 2 less
    than Olly's age. The only pair of numbers that fits these
    conditions is 14 and 12, so **Olly** is **14 years old** and his
    sister is **12 years old**.

Pages 8-9 — 8 and 9 Times Tables

1. **84** should be crossed out. (56 = 7 × 8, 48 = 6 × 8, 36 = 4 × 9)
2. a) 12 × 8 = **96** hills
    b) 12 × 9 = **108** hills
3. 81 ÷ 9 = **9** pages in each chapter
4. 3 × 8 = **24**   10 × 9 = **90**   2 × 8 = 16
    6 × 9 = 54   24 ÷ **8** = 3   27 ÷ 9 = **3**
    64 ÷ 8 = **8**   9 × 9 = **81**   11 × 8 = 88
5. 5 × £8 = £40, and 6 × £8 = £48,
    so the largest number he can afford is **5** notepads.
6. a) 63 ÷ 9 = **7** sips
    b) 8 × 9 = **72** lines

    An Extra Challenge

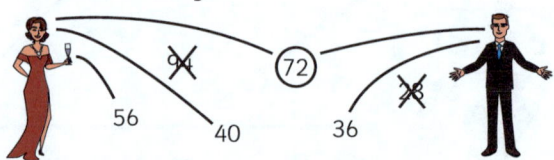

24

Answers

Pages 10-11 — 11 and 12 Times Tables

1. 5 × 11 = **55**   11 × 12 = **132**   6 × 11 = 66
   5 × 12 = 60   **84** ÷ 12 = 7   24 ÷ **12** = 2
   11 × **11** = 121   108 ÷ 12 = **9**   96 ÷ 12 = **8**

2. a) 3 × 12 = **36** oranges
   b) 4 × 11 = 44 pears, so she picks 44 − 36 = **8** more pears.

3. £77 ÷ 11 = £7 per costume.
   So 12 costumes cost £7 × 12 = **£84**.

4. 11 crates is enough for 11 × 12 = 132 bottles, and 10 crates is only enough for 10 × 12 bottles = 120 bottles.
   So Martha will need **11** crates.

5. a) 48 ÷ 12 = 4, so he has 4 lots of 12 chips. He uses 1 pinch for each lot, so he uses 4 × 1 = **4** pinches of salt.
   b) 33 ÷ 11 = 3, so the length of the fish is 3 times the length in the ratio. So multiply the number of drops of vinegar in the ratio by 3 to find the number of drops he uses:
   3 × 12 = **36** drops of vinegar.

An Extra Challenge

Shelly has £22. £22 ÷ 11 = £2, so Mollie has £2 × 12 = **£24**.
Mollie got 144 birthday gifts. 144 ÷ 12 = 12,
so Shelly got 12 × 11 = **132** birthday gifts.
Shelly has 44 friends. 44 ÷ 11 = 4,
so Mollie has 4 × 12 = **48** friends.

Page 12 — Times Tables Challenges 1

1. She must have the same number of small squares along the length and width of the large squares for them to be squares. You can make a large square from 3 × 3 = 9 small squares, and 54 ÷ 9 = 6. So she makes **6 large squares** made up of **9 small squares** each.

2. There are 7 terrapins (Thomasina and her 6 cousins).
   So the terrapins take 7 × 9 = 63 seconds to finish the race.
   84 ÷ 12 = 7, so the race is 7 lots of 12 m.
   So Hugo takes 7 × 11 = 77 seconds to finish.
   63 < 77, so **Thomasina** gets to the finish line first.

3. There are 4 wheels, so there are 4 × 2 = 8 wheel guns per car.
   8 wheel guns + 2 wheel jacks = 10 pieces of equipment per car, which is 8 × 10 = **80 pieces of equipment** in total.
   There are 4 wheels, so there are 4 × 2 = 8 crew members at the wheels. There are 2 × 2 = 4 crew members at the ends of each car, so there are 8 + 4 = 12 crew members per car.
   So there are 8 × 12 = **96 crew members** in total.
   It is 8 × 3 = **24 seconds of work** in total.

Page 13 — Times Tables Challenges 2

1. Comparing frog legs: 10 = 5 × 2, so the medium cauldron has twice as many of each ingredient as the small cauldron. 90 = 10 × 9, so the large cauldron has nine times as many of each ingredient as the medium cauldron.
   So the medium cauldron has 2 × 3 = **6 snails**.
   The small cauldron has 12 ÷ 2 = **6 spiders**,
   and the large cauldron has 9 × 12 = **108 spiders**.
   Finally, the medium cauldron has 72 ÷ 9 = **8 cups of slime** and so the small cauldron has 8 ÷ 2 = **4 cups of slime**.

2. a) The 6-seater roller coaster's maximum capacity must be less than 12 × 6 = 72, and a multiple of 6. The 7-seater roller coaster's maximum capacity must be less than 12 × 7 = 84, and a multiple of 7. Since the maximum capacity is the same for both roller coasters, it must be the highest common multiple of 6 and 7 that is less than 72.
   Multiples of 6: 6, 12, 18, 24, 30, 36, <u>42</u>, 48, 54, 60, 66...
   Multiples of 7: 7, 14, 21, 28, 35, <u>42</u>, 49, 56, 63, 70...
   So the maximum capacity is **42** people.

   b) Macy spent 6 × 2 = 12 tokens on each roller coaster.
   So she rode 60 ÷ 12 = **5** different roller coasters.
   Khalid spent 3 × 2 = 6 tokens on each roller coaster.
   So he rode 60 ÷ 6 = **10** different roller coasters.
   Joe spent 5 × 2 = 10 tokens on each roller coaster.
   So he rode 60 ÷ 10 = **6** different roller coasters.

Pages 14-15 — Mental Calculations

1. To divide by 1000, shift the digits three places to the right:
   £980 ÷ 1000 = **£0.98**.

2. 40 × 9 = **360**   600 × 7 = **4200**
   1080 ÷ 12 = **90**   50 × 90 = **4500**
   660 ÷ 11 = **60**   720 ÷ 80 = **9**

3. 11 × 12 = 132, so 11 × 1.2 = **13.2** pages.

4. 94 = 100 − 6. 100 × 7 = 700, and 6 × 7 = 42.
   So 94 × £7 = £700 − £42 = **£658**.
   (You could also do 90 × £7 + 4 × £7 instead.)

5. 1 hour = 60 minutes. 60 ÷ 10 = 6, so the factory makes 480 ÷ 6 = **80** candles in 10 minutes.

6. a) 18 × 10 = **180** cans
   b) 10 × 10 × 32 = **3200** cans
   c) There are 10 × 10 = 100 cans in a crate.
      100 ÷ 25 = 4, so 100 ÷ 2.5 = 40.
      So it takes her **40 minutes**.

An Extra Challenge

See how each problem is different from Robo-Brain's fact, then adjust the other number that is in the fact.
42 × 6785 = **284 970**   6.785 × 4.2 = **28.497**
            0.042 × 6784 = **284.928**
0.042 × 1 × 6785 = **284.97**   2849.7 ÷ 6785 = **0.42**

Answers

Pages 16-17 — Factors and Multiples

1. Factors of 18: 1 and 18, 2 and 9, 3 and **6**.
2. a) **9   18   27   36   45**
   b) The multiples of 12 are 12, 24, 36, 48...
   36 is also a multiple of 9, so the answer is **36**.
3. 1, **54**   2, **27**   **3**, 18   **6**, 9
4. The factors of 9 are 1, 3 and 9.
   Astrid isn't thinking of 1, and she can't be thinking of 9 since it isn't a factor of 6. 3 is a factor of 6, so she is thinking of **3**.
5. Factors of 132: 1, 2, 3, 4, 6, **11**, 12, **22**, **33**, **44**, **66** and **132**.
   6 of these are multiples of 11.
6. **3 × 4 × 2 × 11** and **4 × 6 × 11** should be circled.
7. There are 5 multiples of 4 between 30 and 50: 32, 36, 40, 44 and 48. So he has 5 teeth on the top row.
   There are 4 multiples of 7 less than 30: 7, 14, 21 and 28. So he has 2 × 4 = 8 teeth on the bottom row.
   This means he has 5 + 8 = **13** teeth in total.

An Extra Challenge

Since both boxes show the same number, Fiona must have said a square number (which is also odd and less than 150). So she could only have said 1, 9, 25, 49, 81 or 121. When the trick repeats, a different factor pair appears, so Fiona's number must have at least 2 different factor pairs (not including 1 and itself, since the boxes never show the number Fiona says). The only number in the list which works is **81** — its factor pairs are: 1 and 81, 3 and 27, 9 and 9.

Pages 18-19 — Squares, Cubes and Primes

1. Microphone: $7^2 = 7 \times 7 =$ **49**, Rabbit: $9^2 = 9 \times 9 =$ **81**,
   Scooter: $12^2 = 12 \times 12 =$ **144**
2. a) **Jess**, **Rupa**, **Liam** and **Chidi** should all be circled as their numbers are prime.
   b) There are **8 primes** less than 20
      (2, 3, 5, 7, 11, 13, 17 and 19).
   c) **97** is the biggest prime less than 100.
3. E.g.:

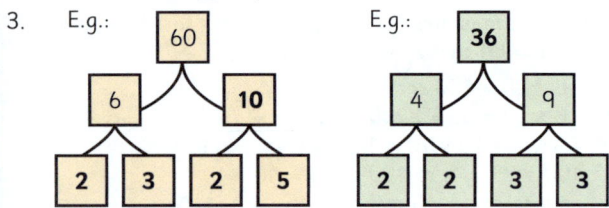

4. a) A: $3^2 =$ **9**, B: $4^2 =$ 16, C: $5^2 =$ **25**
   b) A stack of size A holds $3^3 = 27$ balls, a stack of size B holds $4^3 = 64$ balls, and a stack of size C holds $5^3 = 125$ balls. Look for combinations of 27, 64 and/or 125 that add up to 145: 3 × 27 = 81, and 81 + 64 = 145. So the stacks she uses are: A: **3**, B: **1** and C: **0**.

An Extra Challenge

The number is between $2^3 = 8$ and $3^3 = 27$.
It is one more than a prime, so it must be one of 8, 12, 14, 18, 20 and 24. It can't be 8, because $8^2 = 64$ is not bigger than 100. It also can't be 12, 18 or 24 because they're multiples of 3, so they all have 3 as a factor.
Factors of 14 are 1, 2, 7, and 14 (2 & 7 are prime).
Factors of 20 are 1, 2, 4, 5, 10, and 20 (2 & 5 are prime).
$\frac{1}{2}$ of the factors of 14 are prime, and $\frac{1}{3}$ of the factors of 20 are prime, so the answer must be **20**.

Pages 20-21 — Written Methods

1. 493 × 8 = **3944**   1652 × 7 = **11564**   217 × 4 = **868**   878 × 6 = **5268**

2. a) 4519 ÷ 8 = **564 r 7**   There is a **remainder**, so 564 isn't enough. She needs **565** staff members.
   b) 5252 ÷ 12 = **437 r 8**   There is a **remainder**, so 437 isn't enough. She needs **438** showers.

3. a) 380 × 68 = **25 840**   So there are **25 840** trees.
   b) 25 840 ÷ 8 = **3230**   So **3230** trees should be cut down.
   c) 3230 ÷ 20 = 323 ÷ 2.
      323 ÷ 2 = **161 r 1**   There is a **remainder**, so 161 isn't enough — she needs **162** trucks.
   d) 2253 ÷ 3 = **751**   So each log is **751 cm** long.
   e) 386 ÷ 16 = **24 r 2**
      $\frac{2}{16} = \frac{1}{8}$, so she can cut $24\frac{2}{16}$ or $24\frac{1}{8}$ slices.

An Extra Challenge

714 ÷ 14 = **51** (split this into 5 and 1), 221 ÷ 17 = **13**,
3891 ÷ 8 = 486 r **3**, 288 ÷ 12 = **24**
28 × 280 = **7840** (split this into 7, 8, 4 and 0), 216 ÷ 9 = **24**
1984 ÷ 32 = **62** (split this into 6 and 2)
5 1   13   3 24   7 8 4 0   24   6 2   =   **MATHS RULES OK**!

Pages 22-23 — Race to the Bottom

Boardan: 1 and 64 are both square and cube numbers, but he's practised at least once a week over the year, so the answer must be **64 days**.

Snophelia: 11 is the 5th smallest prime. 11^2 = **121 years old**.

Max: 275 × 14 = **3850**   So he earned **£3850**.

Tefreeza: 510 ÷ 3 = **170**   So she has had **170 dreams**.

Pink: 5 × 12 = **60 doughnuts**

Scarfur: 5 × 7 = 35, so 5 × 0.07 = **0.35 seconds**.

Final Results: 1st: Tefreeza, 2nd: Snophelia, 3rd: Max, 4th: Boardan, 5th: Scarfur, 6th: Pink